MENTAL & EMOTIONAL
DISABILITIES

BY
Jean Dick

EDITED BY
Maythee Kantar

PUBLISHED BY
CRESTWOOD HOUSE
Mankato, MN, U.S.A.

CIP

LIBRARY OF CONGRESS CATALOGING IN PUBLICATION DATA

Dick, Jean.
   Mental and emotional disabilities

   Includes index.
   SUMMARY: Discusses autism, depression, mental retardation, dyslexia, stuttering, hyperactivity, and other disabilities that we are learning more about.
      1. Mental illness—Juvenile literature.   2. Mental retardation—Juvenile literature.   3. Learning disabilities—Juvenile literature. [1. Mentally handicapped. 2. Learning disabilities.] I. Kantar, Maythee. II. Title. III. Series.
RC460.2.M46   1988   616.89—dc19   88-21555
ISBN 0-899686-418-9

International Standard Book Number:	Library of Congress Catalog card Number:
0-89686-418-9	88-21555

PHOTO CREDITS

Cover: Viewfinders: Chris Grajczyk
Viewfinders: (Chris Grajczyk) 16
Taurus Photos: (Martin M. Rotker) 9; (Pam Hasegawa) 39
Globe Photos, Inc.: (Don L. Black) 25, 32-33, 35
Journalism Services/SIU: 26-27, 31
Third Coast Stock Source: (Kent Dufault) 4, 20-21; (William Meyer) 7, 36-37; (MacDonald Photography) 11, 14, 43; (Patrick Dean) 23; (Michael Douglas) 24; (Todd S. Dacqulsto) 40-41; (Phil Krejcarek) 44; (Thomas Lemke) 19
Tom Stack & Associates: (Brian Parker) 29

Produced by Carnival Enterprises.

CRESTWOOD HOUSE

Box 3427, Mankato, MN, U.S.A. 56002

TABLE OF CONTENTS

Many mentally and emotionally disabled children can be helped when they talk to a parent or other adult.

AN INVISIBLE DISABILITY

"Thomas, would you continue reading page six?"

The seven-year-old boy scrambled to his feet. He hadn't been listening, and he wasn't sure of the place.

"The uh- p-p-p," he stammered.

"Pioneers," supplied the teacher.

"The pioneers cr-cr..."

Thomas's ears were burning, and he wished he could sit down. The class snickered. He knew the teacher was irritated. Finally he heard the words he was longing for.

"Sit down, Thomas."

He sank gratefully into his seat, not caring about the impatient look from his teacher, or the mocking faces of his classmates. School, for Thomas A. Edison, was over for another day. It was over forever three months later, when the teacher expelled him, saying he was retarded.

No one knew back in 1854 that this boy who did so poorly in school, who earned bad marks from his teachers and taunts from his peers, would grow up to be a brilliant inventor. No one knew, not even Thomas!

Thomas Edison, like many other intelligent children, had what is now called a *learning disability.* There was something that prevented him from doing well in school.

A learning disability means that there is a difference between a person's intelligence and the way he does his work in school. He gets low marks on the work he turns in and on tests. Many times he gets incomplete or failing grades because he just doesn't do the work at all.

As many as 10% of all Americans have learning disabilities. Most have average or above-average intelligence. Some are even geniuses. They are smart and talented, but for some reason they don't do well in school. They have trouble reading, writing, and doing mathematics. Some have trouble listening, thinking, or paying attention.

Learning disabled boys outnumber girls six to one. Researchers are trying to find out why. Some think there is a connection between *hormones* and learning disabilities. Others look at *heredity* (characteristics received from a person's parents) or injuries.

Hyperactivity, attention deficit disorder, and dyslexia are all learning disabilities. These terms do not mean physical handicaps like deafness or blindness.

All of these problems are similar, however. People with disabilities know they're different. They're often left out of regular social activities or teased. This makes them feel bad. Disabled people have the same needs to be loved as everyone else.

In the past, children with handicaps were ignored

Many people with learning disabilities are smart and talented, but they can't do well in school.

7

and left at home. Some were sent to homes for the retarded. Most were never sent to school. All that has changed. Now our laws require that all disabled children receive a free and appropriate public education. This is called *mainstreaming*, which means moving them into the regular "stream" of life.

ALWAYS IN MOTION

"Knock it off."
"Leave her alone."
"Close that window."
"Can't you sit still for a change?"

Paul heard this, and a lot more, after only one hour of his sixth grade class. He's used to it—Paul has lots of trouble in school. He's smart, but his grades don't show it. He thinks no one likes him.

He's lonely, but he's not alone. Paul is one of millions of children who suffers from a learning disability. Paul's problem is called *attention deficit disorder.*

This problem was first studied more than 100 years ago. Then it was called *hyperactivity.* Even though it has been studied for years, there is much more to learn. No single cause has been found, and there is no single treatment. Children with this disability cannot concentrate on one activity or person for very long.

Experts don't know exactly what causes emotional disabilities.

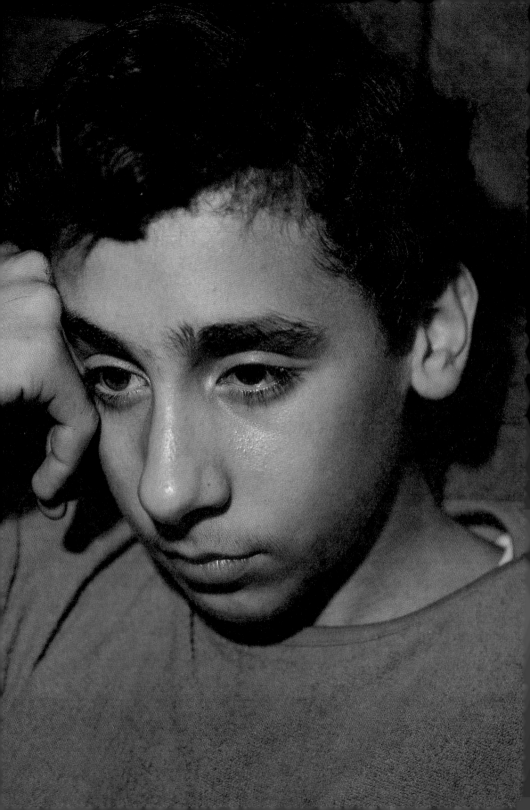

Counseling helps some children. They often go to a *therapist* with their parents. They learn as a family how to cope with this problem. When the parents learn more about attention deficit disorder and understand that the child can't help how he acts, they are able to support him. As they praise his good behavior and help him set limits on his "acting out" behavior, he can begin to like himself more and be easier to live with. Drugs such as *ritalin* are sometimes used to treat this disorder.

Some experts recommend diet changes for children with attention deficit disorder. The Feingold diet, for example, eliminates foods with artificial flavorings or colorings. Some children become less active when they stop eating these foods.

WHEN "COKE" AND "COAT" LOOK THE SAME

Brenda confuses words. "Coat" and "coke" look the same to her. So do "god" and "dog." Is it any wonder she has a hard time reading?

Brenda is frustrated. She can't copy anything from the blackboard. Everything is disorganized. She can't even do the simplest problems. She's ten years old, but she's reading from a third-grade book. She hates

People with dyslexia confuse letters like "b" and "g" and words like "dog" and "god."

leaving her class to study reading with a special education teacher.

Brenda is bright, but she has a problem. It's a learning disability called *dyslexia*. This is the same problem Thomas Edison had. In today's world, however, Brenda has an advantage over Edison. Specially-trained teachers and programs in public schools can help.

When Brenda goes to her reading class she does drills such as tracing letters. Other times she connects broken lines. She learns words and letters through pictures, too. All of this helps her recognize the differences between letters like "b" and "g." With each success, her reading level moves closer to her grade. And as her reading level goes up, her frustration goes down.

TALKING IS HARD WORK

"I d-d-d-d on't r-r-r-r-r emember," Gabriel answered. He was embarrassed. Every time his teacher put him on the spot, he talked like this. Talking in public is hard work for Gabriel.

He suffers from a language problem called *stuttering*. It happens when his vocal muscles don't coordinate. A speech therapist is helping him. She gives him exercises and works hard with him so he will overcome his problem before he graduates.

At least 1 in 30 children stutters at some time. Most outgrow it by age 12. Stuttering almost always goes away by itself. When it doesn't, children like Gabriel can get help.

Most children that stutter speak normally at first. Later they begin to hesitate. If a lot of attention is called to this hesitation, it may get worse. Stress does not cause stuttering, but it can make it worse. This is what happens to Gabriel when his teacher asks him a question. Sometimes stuttering runs in families.

One famous stutterer was Winston Churchill. He overcame his problem and went on to become Prime

Minister of England and a famous public speaker.

Not all stutterers overcome their problem. There are still over two million adults who continue to suffer from some form of stuttering.

Speech and language problems like Gabriel's are very common. Nearly 40 out of every 1,000 children have some type of speech problem.

You've probably heard someone say "yeth" instead of "yes." That's called *lisping*. The "th" sound is spoken instead of "s."

If you hear someone using r, l, t, or d poorly, they are *lalling*. They might say "sik" for "silk."

Someone who says "wabbit" for "rabbit" is *substituting*.

All of these problems can be improved with help from a speech therapist in school.

There is one speech and language problem that is rare and much harder to improve. That is when there is no speech at all. This is called *aphasia*. Sometimes aphasia is caused by a head injury that damages the part of the brain that controls speech. When this happens to young children, therapists work with them to train the other side of the brain to take over this function. "It's very hard work," said one therapist, "but a highly-motivated child can be helped."

If a doctor finds out there is nothing physically wrong, special teachers try to unlock the "prison of silence" children with aphasia live in.

One teacher tried something different. She taught a boy sign language first. Then she urged him to make a sound with each sign. The sounds soon became words. Before long, he dropped the sign language and began to speak. This was just what she had hoped would happen!

UNHAPPY ALL THE TIME

Marie hates school. She hates her teachers. She hates how she looks. In fact, she hates herself. There's only one word to describe her life—unhappy.

Marie doesn't care about anything or anybody. She's even thought about suicide. What's wrong with Marie? She's depressed.

Like a child with a learning disability, Marie is not doing well in school. She used to do well, but since she's been feeling like this, her grades have dropped. She'd rather sleep than do schoolwork. Sometimes she even sleeps in class.

Marie's mother tells her to "shape up." Her teachers think she is lazy. But Marie's problem is more serious than that. *Depression* is something that requires professional help.

Doctors who treat people like Marie will first do some tests to find out what's wrong. A learning disability may be found. Sometimes it's hard to tell

Some teachers use sign language to communicate with disabled children.

which came first—the depression or the learning disability. If a learning disability is found and treated, the depression may go away.

If depression is *diagnosed*, the doctor may suggest counseling or therapy. Many people are helped by talking about their problems with trained therapists. They begin to understand themselves better and learn new ways of dealing with problems. Sometimes they are alone with the counselor. Other times they are in group counseling with others like them or with their families. Drugs are also prescribed for depressed children. *Lithium* is one common anti-depressant drug.

Therapy, counseling, and medicine can help children overcome depression. With time, the pain that is part of being constantly unhappy can go away.

A LONG HISTORY OF FAILING

Joe is 12 and he already has a long history of failing. In fact, he can't remember anything else. Joe thinks of himself as bad and he acts that way. He kicks and punches and yells and has temper tantrums at home and at school. Then he wonders why no one likes him. He doesn't feel right at school parties or

Many people have a hard time recovering from a low feeling called depression.

other social events that his parents want him to attend.

Joe gets angry and aggressive like other children his age. But Joe's anger and behavior go beyond what's normal because they interfere with his learning and daily life. Joe is *emotionally disturbed*. About 12 out of every 1,000 boys and girls are, too.

Experts don't know exactly what causes emotional disturbances. Some say it begins early in life with poor family relationships when parents fight all the time. Sometimes parents are too strict, or too lenient about their child's behavior. Some experts think that a home where parents are abusing drugs or alcohol can bring on emotional disturbances, too.

Other experts play down the importance of the parents' behavior and say that emotional disturbances are inherited.

Whatever the causes, emotionally disturbed children do not develop in a healthy way. They feel awful inside and fear failure. Some give up trying anything, and most are negative about everything and everybody. They express their feelings in harmful ways.

Like Marie, Joe can get help. After a careful diagnosis, his treatment begins. He goes to a therapist once a week to talk about his problems. His parents and teachers help him, too. They encourage his good behavior. They help him develop his artistic talents with special art lessons.

Teachers may encourage good behavior of disabled children by using special art lessons.

Occasionally, a child like Joe is found to have a learning disability. As with depressed children, when the learning disability is treated the emotional problems may begin to disappear.

BLIND WHILE SEEING, DEAF WHILE HEARING

Sam sits alone in the corner. He doesn't talk or react to anything that's going on. He can't stand to look anyone in the eye. He'd rather stare at a jigsaw puzzle

19

Many times a therapist can help a disabled child talk through his or her problems.

all day long. He has withdrawn into a world of his own.

Like Paul and Brenda, Sam has normal intelligence. But unlike them, he is not mainstreamed. This is because Sam's problem is severe. Sam is suffering from *autism.* Until he gets better, he'll stay in special education classes.

In the past, people thought children like Sam couldn't be taught at all. Now parents and teachers are moving into their private worlds. Programs that take hundreds of hours of loving care are helping. Seven days a week, 10 or 12 hours a day, parents, teachers, and friends work with the autistic child using music, games, and touching. Slowly, they enter the child's private world and the child begins to react. After that first reaction, many autistic children move steadily into the world. "They have to climb mountains," said one parent, "to do what other children accomplish easily."

Autism is a very puzzling emotional disability. Again, four times as many boys have this disability. There are two to five cases of autism for every 10,000 children. Researchers are trying to learn more about these children who are "blind while seeing, deaf while hearing." They hope to find new ways to help them overcome their disability and live happy, healthy lives.

A SPECIAL HEARTACHE

Children like the ones you've read about often ask themselves, "Why wasn't I invited?" "Won't I ever have any friends?" They want to be accepted and included in social events.

Some kids find a way to be accepted. They do very well in music or art or sports.

Former Olympic medal winner Greg Louganis has a disability. When he was in grade school, people said he was lazy. Some called him dumb. He got poor grades and he felt awful inside.

Then Greg learned he had special talents. By the age of ten, he could dance and dive better than anyone in

Invisible disabilities like dyslexia are hard for teachers to recognize.

his class. He practiced constantly. "I didn't have anything else," Greg said later.

When Greg got to high school, he practiced and improved his diving. His grades, however, did not improve. He got C's and D's. "I honestly thought I was retarded," he said, "because diving was the only thing I could do well." And he did do well! In the 1984 Olympics he won a gold medal.

At age 18, Greg enrolled at the University of Miami. His problem with schoolwork continued. But this time, Greg found out what was wrong. He was dyslexic. Now he could get the special help he needed to develop his other talents.

Once a disability is discovered, teachers can work with students to overcome them.

126,000 children born each year are mentally retarded.

ALWAYS SLOWER

Linda is a friendly, happy child. She smiles a lot and is easy to be around. She enjoys life and has a good sense of humor. Like Gabriel, who stutters, Linda doesn't do well in school. She's 12 years old but she's reading a first-grade book.

There's a difference between Linda and Gabriel, though. Linda does not have normal intelligence. Linda is one of the 126,000 children born each year who is *mentally retarded.*

When she was little, Linda was always slower than her brother. She didn't grab things, sit up, or walk

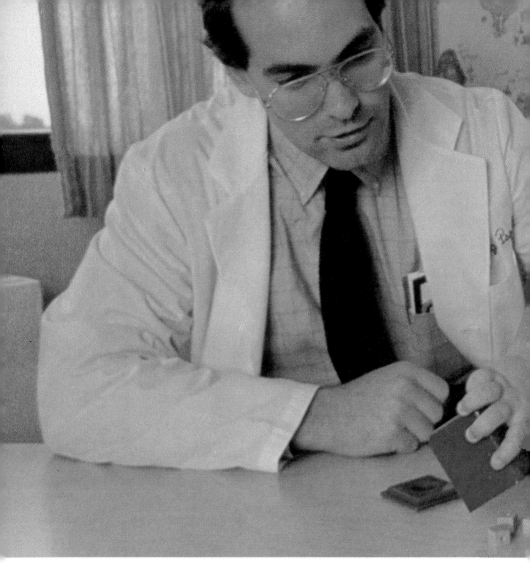

Doctors can test children and find out their "intelligent quotient."

when her parents expected her to. At first they thought she would catch up. She didn't. When Linda was four, the family doctor tested her. He found that Linda has an IQ of 68. She is retarded, but she can go to school and learn.

IQ stands for *Intelligence Quotient*. People with IQs over 100 are considered normal. Linda is in the *educable* class of 55 to 69. Children are considered *borderline* if their IQ is 70 to 84. Those with IQs of 85 to 100 are called *slow learners*. All of these children can learn and are mainstreamed. What they learn varies from child to child and cannot be predicted by IQ scores. "We've found too often," said one teacher, "that low expectations result in low performance."

Why is Linda retarded? There are many answers to that question. Sometimes mental retardation is inherited. Infection or disease in the pregnant mother can cause retardation. So can a blow to the head or an injury at birth. Research shows that poor nutrition can cause retardation, too. New methods of helping retarded children are being developed as more is learned about this disability.

Linda knows she is different than the other students in her regular classes. When they laugh or call her "retard," she hurts inside. Just like children with learning disabilities, adolescence is a particularly hard time for her. She's experiencing the same physical changes as all 12-year-olds, but she's not growing mentally at the same rate.

In the past, many retarded children were put into state homes. They were cared for, but not taught reading, writing, or math. Now they are mainstreamed into gym, art, and music classes. They attend special classes for reading, writing, and math.

Being able to read and write has opened up the world for Linda. She can read bus signs and get around the city. She can take her mother's shopping

The Special Olympics are held for mentally disabled children.

list to the store and bring home a few groceries. When she finishes school, Linda hopes to find a job. Someday she may live on her own and support herself.

In the past, many retarded adults worked in *sheltered workshops.* These are places set up to provide jobs for disabled people. They might do simple tasks like putting together packages or stuffing envelopes.

Now more and more mentally retarded people are working in more demanding jobs. Disabled people are being mainstreamed into the workplace just as they were mainstreamed into the classroom. They're finding success there, too.

PARENTS HAVE PROBLEMS, TOO

Most parents of a disabled child have suspected a problem in their son or daughter. They wait and see, hoping the problem will go away. When it doesn't, they usually take the child to their family doctor for an examination. If the doctor tells them their child isn't "normal," they react in many ways. Some are embarrassed. "Why did this happen to us?" Others get angry. Some just don't believe it.

When parents begin to accept the diagnosis, they

ask a lot of questions. "What did we do wrong?" "Could this have been prevented?" "Will he ever be normal?" "What can we do now?"

Family doctors and school counselors or therapists are happy to answer these questions. Some get groups of parents of disabled children together. The parents talk about their concerns and their children and learn from each other.

One counselor advises parents, "Let your children

Researchers, doctors, teachers, and parents work together to find the answers to mental, emotional, and learning disabilities.

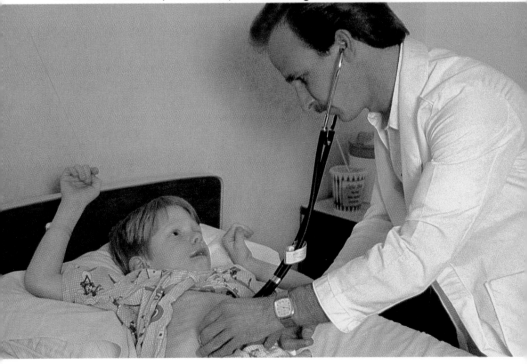

With support and encouragement, people with disabilities can succeed at anything.

be children." She said disabled children had enough problems being disabled without being criticized at home all the time.

Another counselor said, "Treat your children

according to the age they act, not the age they are."

Counselors also ask parents to encourage their children. "Support them in what they do well," one said. Greg Louganis is a good example of a dyslexic child whose parents encouraged his interest in diving.

Some parents are helped by attending counseling

with their child. Others get involved in behavior modification programs at home. This is a way of changing behavior with a system of rewards and punishments. Parents and teachers often work together on this. At home, parents work out a step-by-step program for the child. If the child does not have a tantrum, for example, he will be allowed to watch television for an hour. At school, the teacher may reward assignments turned in on time with bonus points worth prizes. Punishments are part of the program, too. That could mean an evening without television, or staying an hour after school.

Parents should remember they are not alone. Even laws are there to help. Since 1975, Public Law 94-142 guarantees their child an equal education. This can mean special teachers or even private help. Disabled children have made great progress when parents and teachers work together to help them.

A TEACHER TELLS HER STORY

Many disabled children begin school without knowing what is wrong with them. When that happens, teachers often ask parents to have children tested. Schools offer free assessment, too. When physical problems are ruled out, a diagnosis of

Many children with disabilities are successfully "mainstreamed" into gym, art, and music classes.

34

A teacher encourages her class of special education students.

learning, emotional, or mental disability may be made. That's when special education teachers come in. One teacher told this story:

"The special education students I teach are more like regular students than different. They have lots of

talents and abilities. I develop a program for each one of them. Then they can move at their own speed. It's wonderful to watch their progress. They feel so good when they succeed. So do I! Sure, progress is slow. Sometimes they even go backwards for a while. But they move ahead over time.

"These children will probably always struggle. With help, though, most of them will be in a full day of classes before long. We let them be normal here, and we urge parents to do the same. The other special teachers and I never forget every child has potential."

HOW WOULD YOU FEEL

Have you ever thought how you would feel if you had a disability? Do you ever wonder what it would be like? How would it feel to be left out? What if someone called you names?

These are just a few questions that may help you put yourself in Gabriel's or Linda's place. If someone is in a wheelchair, you can see he or she is disabled and you might try to offer help if it were needed. But it's not so easy to see that someone with a learning or emotional disability needs help. These invisible disabilities can be easier to live with if you are understanding and caring.

One student approached a learning disabled classmate this way. He told him he would like to invite him to a party at his home, but he didn't want to be embarrassed by a tantrum. Then he worked out a

Children with mental, emotional, and learning disabilities need a lot of understanding and caring.

38

Researchers are constantly looking for ways to treat and prevent disabilities.

signal with his classmate so he could let him know if he was acting up too much. Everything worked out fine and the boy who had always been left out began to be included in more activities outside of the classroom.

SPEAKING OUT

Greg Louganis is just one star who is speaking out about his problem. He hopes going public will help others understand and get help. Former Olympic decathlon star Bruce Jenner is also talking about dyslexia, which is his disability too. So is actor Tom Cruise, saying he made up for his dyslexia by becoming a good actor. Newspaper advertisements picturing the late Sir Winston Churchill with the headline, "Stuttering didn't stop Winston Churchill," offer encouragement to stutterers.

Radio, television, and newspapers are spreading the message about disabilities to everyone. It's no longer a big secret—something to be ashamed of. Schools and libraries provide information, too. There are books and magazines full of information about every kind of disability and about groups that provide support. YMCAs and YWCAs offer special programs, as well as summer camps, for disabled children.

Colleges and universities have developed programs

that include group counseling and tutoring. There are special study-skills classes for those that need them. Some schools even offer special entrance examinations.

Self-help groups are springing up in communities all over the country. The Association of Learning Disabled Adults is one of them.

Researchers are working, too. They want to know what causes disabilities so they can find out how to

Study-skills and self-help classes help people live active and independent lives.

treat them. Better yet, they want to learn how to prevent them.

Researchers, doctors, teachers, and parents working together are trying to find answers. They all hope disabled children will overcome their disabilities and become healthy adults. One child who's on his way said, "Now I've learned to use words, not my fists."

A disability does not have to prevent anyone from making friends and being happy.

FOR MORE INFORMATION

For more information about mental, emotional, and learning disabilities, write to:

The Foundation for Children with Learning
    Disabilities
99 Park Avenue
Sixth Floor
New York, NY 10016

The Association for Children and Adults with
    Learning Disabilities
4156 Library Road
Pittsburgh, PA 15234

GLOSSARY/INDEX

APHASIA 13—*A partial or complete failure to use language.*

ATTENTION DEFICIT DISORDER 6, 8, 10—*A learning disability. The person suffering from it may be hyperactive or impulsive.*

COUNSELING 10, 17, 33, 43 — *A professional service designed to help a person better understand his or her problems.*

DEPRESSION 15, 17, 19—*A mental disorder when a person is very sad and feels that he or she is a failure. The person suffering feels negative about himself or herself. Sometimes the person tries to commit suicide.*

DIAGNOSIS 17, 30 — *Identifying a disease or condition after observing its signs and symptoms.*

DYSLEXIA 6, 11, 24, 33, 42—*A learning disability that results in severe reading problems.*

EMOTIONALLY DISTURBED 18 — *A complex disorder that results in behavior that isn't acceptable.*

HEREDITY 6 — *Characteristics that a child gets from his parents or ancestors.*

HORMONES 6—*A product of a person's cells that controls various body functions when it is released into the blood stream. One of the most important hormones regulates development.*

HYPERACTIVITY 6, 8—*Very active; unable to stay still for a long period of time.*

GLOSSARY/INDEX

INTELLIGENCE QUOTIENT 26, 27 — *(IQ) An estimate of learning potential determined by a standard test.*

LALLING 13 — *A language problem where someone uses r, l, t, or d poorly in speech.*

LEARNING DISABILITY 5, 6, 15, 17, 19, 38 — *A term used to describe a condition when there is a difference between a person's performance and his or her intelligence.*

LISPING 13 — *A language problem where the person does not pronounce s and z properly. They may sound like "th."*

LITHIUM 17 — *One of many drugs used to treat depression.*

MAINSTREAMING 8, 22, 28, 30 — *A way of putting disabled and non-disabled people together according to their educational needs.*

MENTALLY RETARDED 5, 8, 24, 25, 28, 30 — *Slowness in mental growth compared to others of the same age.*

RITALIN 10 — *A drug sometimes used to treat people suffering from attention deficit disorder.*

STUTTERING 12, 13, 25, 42 — *A speech problem in which a person hesitates and rapidly repeats letters or words or has breathing spasms.*

SUBSTITUTION 13 — *A speech problem in which a*

GLOSSARY/INDEX

person replaces one letter with another.

THERAPIST 10, 12, 13, 17, 31—*A person who specializes in the treatment of mental or emotional disorders.*

VOCAL MUSCLES 12—*Muscles in the throat used to produce sound.*